DATE DUE

WITHDRAWN FROM EVLD

HorrorScapes

Tut's Deadly Tomb

by Natalie Lunis

Consultant: Nicholas Reeves, Ph.D.
Egyptologist and author of
The Complete Tutankhamun:
The King, the Tomb, the Royal Treasure

BEARPORT
PUBLISHING

New York, New York

Credits

Cover and Title Page illustration, Dawn Beard Creative and Kim Jones; 4–5, Kim Jones; 6, © Rue des Archives/ The Granger Collection, New York; 7, © The Granger Collection, New York; 8, © When They Were Young: The Boy King of Egypt, Jackson, Peter (1922–2003)/Private Collection/© Look and Learn/The Bridgeman Art Library International; 9L, © Robert Harding Picture Library/SuperStock; 9R, © Robert Harding Picture Library/SuperStock; 10, © Hulton Archive/Getty Images; 11T, © North Wind Picture Archives/Alamy; 11B, © The Granger Collection, New York; 12, © Bridgeman Art Library/SuperStock; 13L, © Robert Harding Picture Library/SuperStock; 13R, © Robert Harding Picture Library/SuperStock; 14, © Robert Harding Picture Library/ SuperStock; 15T, © Frank Miesnikowicz/Alamy; 15B, © Robert Harding Picture Library/SuperStock; 16, © Brad Walker/SuperStock; 17, © Art Media/Imagestate/Photolibrary; 18L, © Robert Harding Picture Library/SuperStock; 18C, © Robert Harding Picture Library/SuperStock; 18R, © Robert Harding Picture Library/SuperStock; 19, © ullstein bild/The Granger Collection; 20, Kim Jones; 21L, © The Sandusky Register, Tuesday April 10, 1923/ Newspaper Archive; 21R, © Moberly Monitor–Index, Monday December 2, 1935/Newspaper Archive; 22L, © Griffith Institute, University of Oxford; 22R, © Rue des Archives/The Granger Collection, New York; 23, © Everett Collection, Inc.; 24, © World History Archive/Newscom; 25T, © Hulton Archive/Getty Images; 25B, © Rue des Archives/The Granger Collection, New York; 26, © Philip and Karen Smith/SuperStock; 27L, © AP Images/Ben Curtis; 27R, © Cris Bouroncle/AFP/Newscom; 28, © Bruno Perousse/age fotostock/SuperStock; 29, © Supreme Council for Antiquities/Reuters/Landov; 31, © Jose Antonio Sanchez/Shutterstock; 32, © Sue C/Shutterstock.

Publisher: Kenn Goin
Editorial Director: Adam Siegel
Creative Director: Spencer Brinker
Design: Dawn Beard Creative and Kim Jones
Illustrations: Kim Jones
Photo Researcher: Picture Perfect Professionals, LLC

Library of Congress Cataloging-in-Publication Data

Lunis, Natalie.
  Tut's deadly tomb / by Natalie Lunis ; consultant, Nicholas Reeves.
     p. cm. — (Horrorscapes)
  Includes bibliographical references and index.
  ISBN-13: 978-1-936087-98-3 (library binding)
  ISBN-10: 1-936087-98-7 (library binding)
  1. Tutankhamen, King of Egypt—Tomb—Juvenile literature. 2. Blessing and cursing—
Egypt—Juvenile literature. I. Reeves, C. N. (Carl Nicholas), 1956– II. Title.
  DT87.5.L865 2011
  932'.014092—dc22

                              2010008025

For more information, write to Bearport Publishing Company, Inc., 101 Fifth Avenue, Suite 6R, New York, New York 10003. Printed in the United States of America in North Mankato, Minnesota.

062010
042110CGC

10 9 8 7 6 5 4 3 2 1

Contents

Opening the Tomb

Howard Carter picked up an iron rod and chipped away at part of a heavy stone door. His friend, Lord Carnarvon, stood close by in the underground passageway. Both men knew by now that the doorway led farther into the **tomb** of Tutankhamun (*too*-tahn-KAH-muhn), a king of ancient Egypt. However, they did not know what they would find on the other side.

Before entering the tomb, Howard Carter and his crew had spent days digging out the steps that led to the tomb's underground entrance.

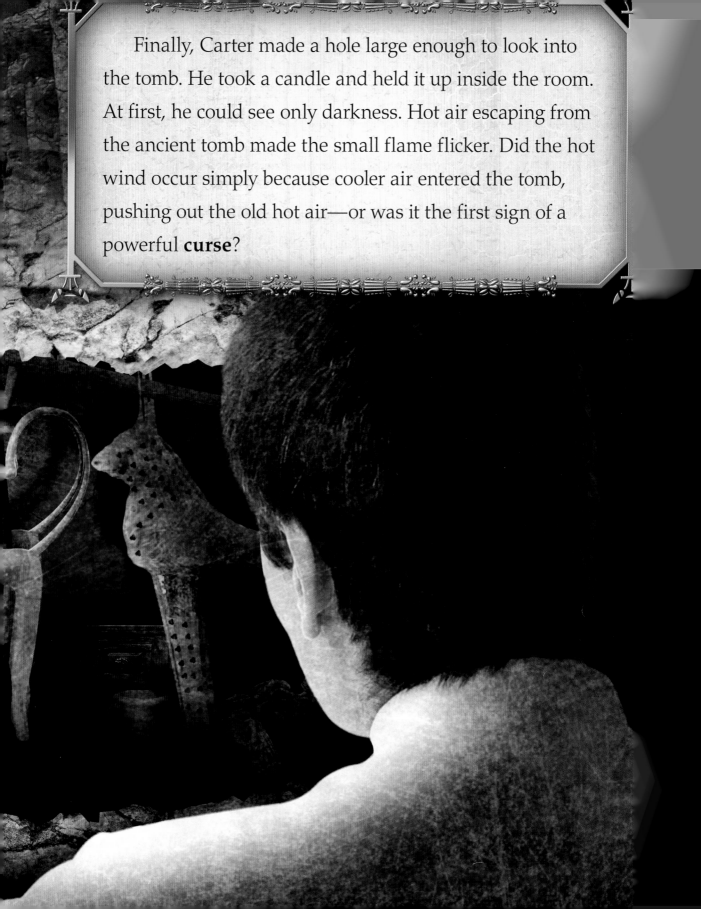

Finally, Carter made a hole large enough to look into the tomb. He took a candle and held it up inside the room. At first, he could see only darkness. Hot air escaping from the ancient tomb made the small flame flicker. Did the hot wind occur simply because cooler air entered the tomb, pushing out the old hot air—or was it the first sign of a powerful **curse**?

Wonderful Things!

Howard Carter had been searching for King Tutankhamun's tomb for years. In 1909, the **archaeologist** began working for Lord Carnarvon, a wealthy Englishman who was fascinated by ancient Egypt. He had hired Carter to explore and dig in places that might hold tombs and **temples** from the rich and powerful Egyptian kingdom. Now, 13 years later, on November 26, 1922, the two men were closer than ever to a spectacular find.

Lord Carnarvon (left) and Howard Carter (right) outside Tutankhamun's tomb

Lord Carnarvon became interested in the ancient art and history of Egypt after traveling there for his health. He found that the sunny, warm Egyptian winters were better for him than the cold,

As Carter held the candle inside Tut's tomb, Lord Carnarvon waited. When he could not stand the **suspense** any longer, he asked if Carter could see anything. Carter could hardly speak but managed to reply, "Yes, wonderful things!" Among them were gold statues and gold pieces of furniture. There were also other beautiful works of art—all belonging to a young king who had been dead for more than 3,000 years.

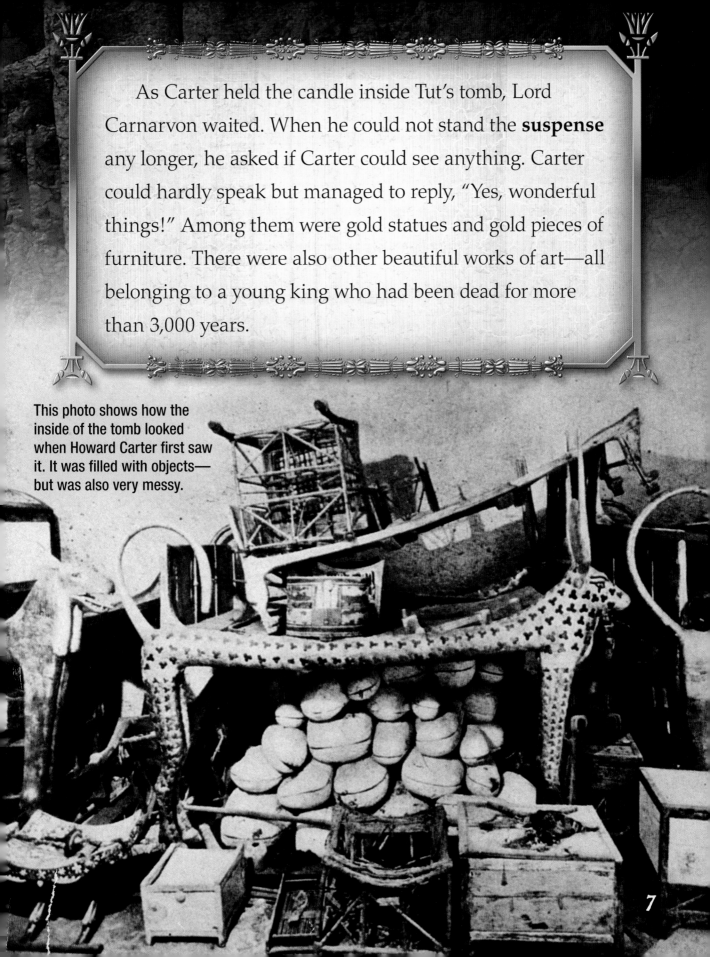

This photo shows how the inside of the tomb looked when Howard Carter first saw it. It was filled with objects—but was also very messy.

The Boy King

King Tutankhamun is often called by the shorter name "King Tut." He is also known as "the boy king" because he became the **pharaoh** of Egypt at the age of nine.

This illustration shows how the young ruler may have looked.

Tut took the throne around 1332 B.C., a few years after his father, King Akhenaten (*ah*-ken-AHT-en), died. However, the young pharaoh ruled Egypt for only a brief time. Tut was dead by the age of 18 or 19. He did not have a son to take his place. Instead, an adviser to Tut called Ay (EYE), who was also probably a relative, named himself the new pharaoh.

This scene shows King Tut driving a chariot.

A sculpture of King Tut's head

No one knows why King Tut died so young. Years ago, some **experts** thought he was murdered. Today, however, many experts think that he died as the result of either a disease or an injury—or both.

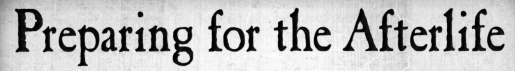

Preparing for the Afterlife

In order to become the new pharaoh, Ay had to first bury Tutankhamun, the pharaoh who came before him. The Egyptians had complex burial **customs** and a deep belief in the **afterlife**, so the task ahead was huge.

A grand tomb was usually built for a pharaoh during his lifetime so that it would be ready when he died. Because of Tut's early death, however, there had not been enough time to build one. Instead, Ay found a smaller tomb. It was made up of a passageway and four rooms. He had it prepared for the boy king.

The dry, empty valley where Tutankhamun's tomb is located is known as the Valley of the Kings. In ancient times, more than 30 Egyptian kings were buried in this area.

Artists decorated the walls of Tut's tomb with prayers and spells from the **Book of the Dead**, a text that served as a guide to the afterworld. Helpers collected statues, pieces of furniture, jewelry, and clothing, as well as dishes, cups, and food. All these were things that Egyptians believed a person would need in the afterlife.

Part of the Book of the Dead recorded on papyrus

Many kinds of food—including meat, beans, fruit, honey, and spices—were placed in the tomb in containers like these.

The Book of the Dead was not an actual book made up of pages and a cover. Its prayers and spells were recorded on the walls of tombs or on long rolls of papyrus, a kind of paper made from the strong stems of a water plant.

11

Making a Mummy

According to ancient Egyptian beliefs, King Tut—like all pharaohs—was considered a living god. After his death on Earth, he would continue his life in the afterworld among the other gods. However, like any other person, Tut needed his body for life in the afterworld. In order to keep the young pharaoh's body from rotting, highly skilled **embalmers** started working on it soon after his death. They took the steps that were needed to make it into a **mummy**.

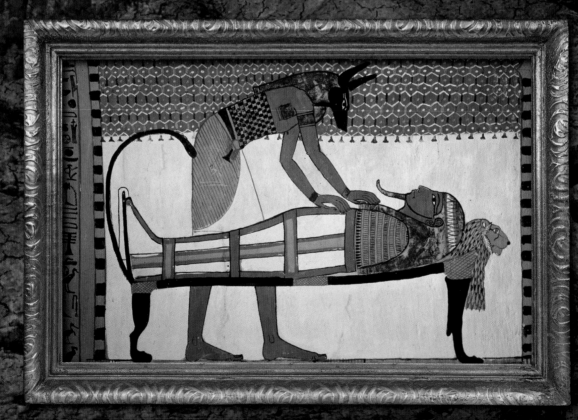

The ancient Egyptians had many gods. One of them was Anubis, the god of death and embalmers. He was usually shown with the head of a kind of wild dog called a jackal. Anubis is pictured here preparing a mummy.

First, four **internal organs**—the lungs, liver, intestines, and stomach—were removed, dried, and placed in special containers. The brain was also removed, but it was thrown away. The Egyptians did not believe it had an important use. The body was then placed in a bed of salt. It remained there for 40 days while the salt drew water from the body and dried it out. Finally, the dried body was wrapped in cloth. It was now a mummy, ready for burial.

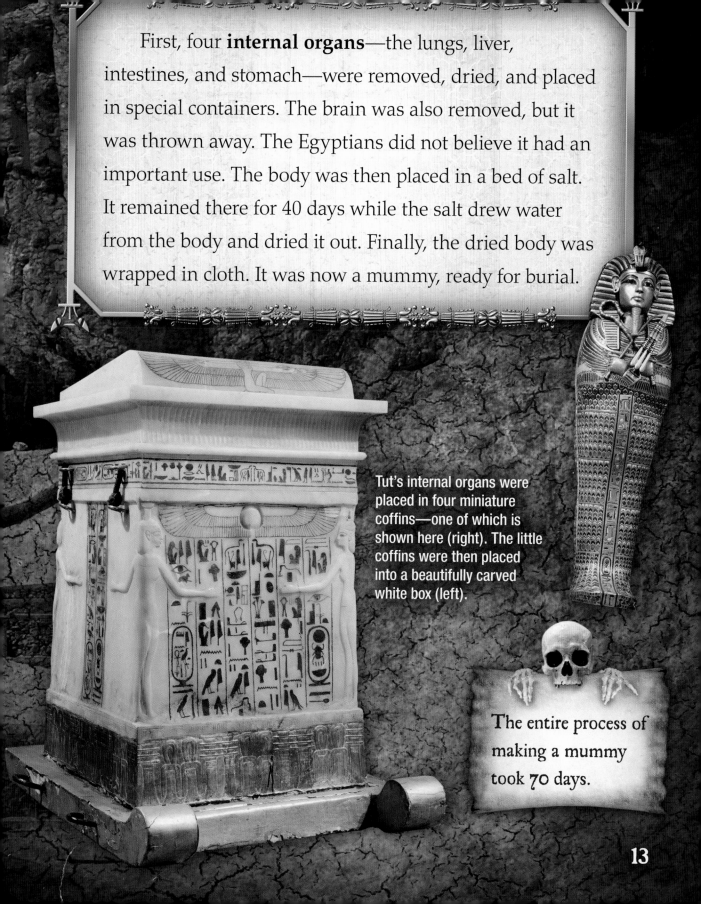

Tut's internal organs were placed in four miniature coffins—one of which is shown here (right). The little coffins were then placed into a beautifully carved white box (left).

The entire process of making a mummy took 70 days.

Sealed Forever

A simple tomb may have been chosen for King Tut, but in every other way he received a burial that was fit for a great king. His mummy was covered by a magnificent gold mask and placed in a solid gold coffin. It was then carried to the tomb, where a priest performed a ceremony called the Opening of the Mouth.

Tut's gold mask

During the ceremony, a priest touched **sacred** objects to the mummy's mouth, eyes, and nose. Now, it was believed, the mummy would be able to breathe, eat, drink, and enjoy life in the afterworld. It could at last be left inside the tomb, along with all its treasures. The doors of the tomb could then be **sealed** forever.

Inside the **burial chamber**, King Tut's mummy and gold coffin were enclosed in two more gold coffins and a stone case called a **sarcophagus**.

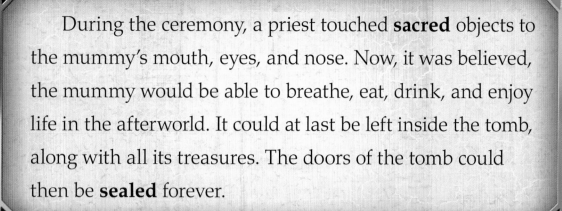

King Tut's sarcophagus

All three of King Tut's coffins were shaped and decorated to look like his body.

15

Tomb Builders and Tomb Robbers

For more than a thousand years before Tut's death, Egyptians had been burying their kings in splendid tombs. At first, the tombs were huge, aboveground **pyramids**. Unfortunately, tomb robbers stole the treasures from many of these pyramids. As a result, starting around 1500 B.C., builders began carving underground tombs out of the rocky earth in the area now known as the Valley of the Kings. These tombs were designed to be completely hidden.

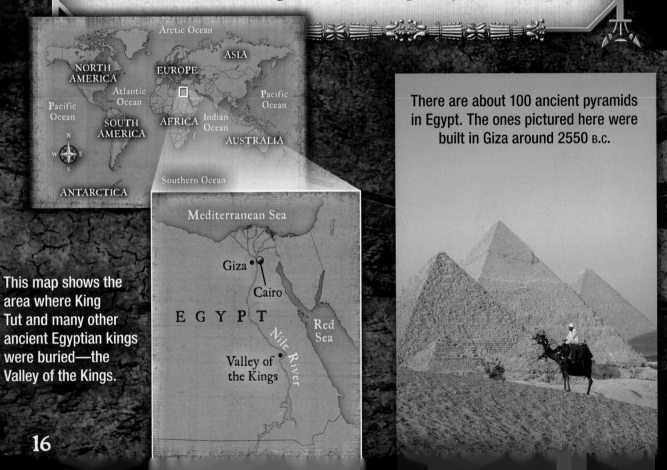

This map shows the area where King Tut and many other ancient Egyptian kings were buried—the Valley of the Kings.

There are about 100 ancient pyramids in Egypt. The ones pictured here were built in Giza around 2550 B.C.

Despite the builders' efforts, however, the underground tombs were robbed as well. In fact, when Howard Carter first discovered Tut's underground tomb, he could tell that it had been broken into twice. He could also tell that both break-ins had occurred not long after Tut's burial. That meant that whatever was left inside the tomb had not been disturbed for more than 3,000 years.

The messiness inside King Tut's tomb suggested that robbers had entered and searched for pieces of gold and other precious items.

The ancient Egyptians looked upon tomb robbery as a very serious crime. Tomb robbers who were caught were put to death.

An Ancient Curse

In the days and weeks that followed their first look into Tut's tomb, Howard Carter and Lord Carnarvon went on to uncover a great deal more. They made a large hole and entered the room that was piled high with "wonderful things." Once inside, they examined its treasures up close. They also found that three more rooms lay beyond the first one. The most exciting discovery of all was that one of them seemed to be Tutankhamun's burial chamber. Would Tut's mummy still be resting there?

These beautiful objects were discovered in Tut's tomb.

Newspapers around the world followed the story with great excitement. However, on April 5, 1923, the story took a dark turn. After an illness that had begun several weeks earlier, Lord Carnarvon was dead. Now many people began to ask if an ancient curse was to blame.

A painting of the *Titanic* sinking

Even before the discovery of Tut's tomb, there was talk of "the mummy's curse." Some people blamed the 1912 sinking of the *Titanic*, a giant ocean liner, on a mummy that was being carried on board. In fact, however, there was no mummy on the ship.

19

More Victims

Lord Carnarvon's death wasn't the only sign that a curse might be at work. In Cairo (KYE-roh)—the Egyptian city where Lord Carnarvon died—a power failure occurred at the exact moment of his death, causing all the lights to go out. Also, at the very same time but thousands of miles away, another strange thing occurred. Lord Carnarvon's dog, a fox terrier named Susie, howled once and then fell down dead.

Howard Carter had a pet canary. Shortly before he discovered Tut's tomb, however, it was killed by a cobra—which is a symbol of the kings of ancient Egypt. Many people came to feel that the canary's death was a sign of the curse that was about to strike.

By 1929, the deaths of more people were also linked to the curse. All of them were involved in one way or another with the discovery of the tomb. They were all also said to be the victims of a **vengeful** pharaoh who did not want his mummy disturbed or his treasures taken away.

Many stories about the curse appeared in newspapers.

Some newspaper stories reported that the curse was recorded on a stone **tablet** in Tut's tomb. The words on the tablet were: "Death shall come on swift wings to him that touches the tomb of Pharaoh."

Fact or Fiction?

After Lord Carnarvon died, Howard Carter continued to explore and study the tomb. In 1925, he found Tutankhamun's mummy and unwrapped it. As the work went on, he did not die. Yet neither did the stories about the curse.

King Tut's mummy

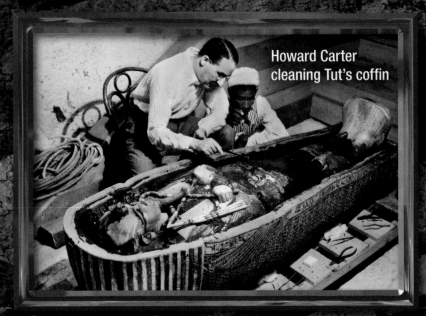

Howard Carter cleaning Tut's coffin

As rumors of the mummy's curse spread, some **collectors** in Europe and the United States feared that their Egyptian **artifacts** would bring bad luck. As a result, they hurried to get rid of them.

Was the curse real? Many people at the time believed it was. Others, however, including Carter himself, believed the stories about the curse were based on **superstition**. They pointed out details that were untrue. For example, the stone tablet supposedly bearing the curse never existed. It was simply made up—perhaps to sell more newspapers.

Mummies have been a popular subject for many horror movies.
This poster was created for a movie that was made in 1932.

A Deadly Mold?

Besides **supernatural** forces, what else could have caused the high number of deaths among those who entered Tut's tomb? Some people have offered a scientific explanation. They think that deadly **bacteria** or **molds** might have been sealed inside the tomb. These **toxins** might have been growing in the foods that were left for the pharaoh. Perhaps Lord Carnarvon and the other "victims" became ill and died after breathing in or touching the ancient but still powerful substances.

Had a deadly toxin been growing in the tomb since the time it was sealed?

Others who doubt the curse have a far simpler explanation. They have compared the pattern of deaths to the pattern that could be expected for a normal group of people and found little difference. In their view, nothing out of the ordinary happened—except for the discovery of extraordinary things from the ancient past.

Howard Carter lived for a long time after the opening of the tomb in 1922. Carter died in 1939, at the age of 64.

Some think that people who entered Tut's tomb died because the Egyptians used poisons from plants or from scorpions and snakes to "booby-trap" important tombs. Anyone who entered one would come into contact with the substances and die.

People who do not believe in the curse point out that an infected mosquito bite probably caused the illness that led to Lord Carnarvon's death.

25

Tut Today

Some who took part in the opening of King Tut's tomb died soon after the event. Others, however, went on to live long lives. What happened to King Tut and his treasures?

Today, thousands of tourists from around the world visit King Tut's tomb each month. Thousands more, such as this boy, view his treasures at the Egyptian Museum in Cairo.

The pharaoh's treasures were moved to the Egyptian Museum in Cairo after their discovery. King Tut's mummy, however, has always been too **fragile** to be moved. It has remained where it was found—inside its tomb in the Valley of the Kings. Now one of Egypt's most important sights, the tomb has been visited by millions of people from all over the world. As far as anyone knows, none of them have been stricken by a curse . . . at least not yet!

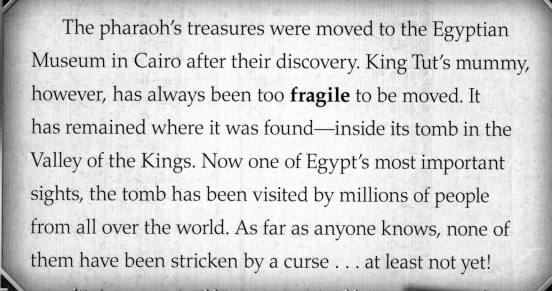

The head of King Tut's mummy

Scientists continue to study Tut's mummy, both to learn more about it and to find ways to prevent damage to it as time goes on.

King Tut's tomb is the only pharaoh's tomb that has ever been found looking close to the way it was left behind after a burial. All the other tombs found so far were emptied by robbers.

EGYPT:
Then and Now

Then: At the time of King Tut's burial, Egypt was a rich and powerful kingdom. About 3 million people lived there. Already almost 2,000 years old, it was one of the world's first civilizations.

Now: About 80 million people live in Egypt. Cairo, its capital city, is the largest city in Africa.

The city of Cairo today

Then: Egypt was ruled by a king known as the pharaoh. When a pharaoh died, his oldest son became the new ruler.

Now: Egypt is governed by a president, who is elected by voters. Voters also elect a group of national representatives known as the People's Assembly.

Then: Egyptians had many gods in their religion. Among them were Ra, the sun god, and Anubis, the god of death.

Now: Most Egyptians—about 90 percent—are Muslim. Christians are the second-largest religious group.

Then: Egyptians buried their pharaohs in a dry, rocky valley that they called the Great Place. The pharaoh's tombs were cut into the earth and had hidden entrances to keep robbers away.

Now: More than 60 tombs have been found in the Great Place, known today as the Valley of the Kings. Thousands of tourists visit each week.

Then: Embalmers preserved bodies as mummies. They used materials such as salt, sap from trees, mud from the Nile River, and linen cloth in their work.

Now: Scientists study the preserved bodies using high-tech equipment such as computers and CT scanners.

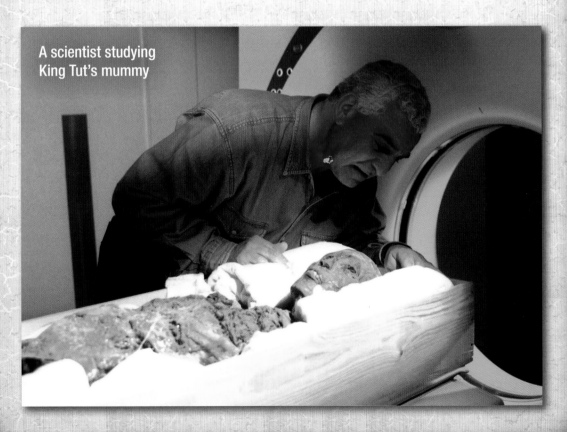
A scientist studying King Tut's mummy

Glossary

afterlife (AF-tur-*life*) the life a person has after he or she dies

archaeologist (*ar*-kee-OL-uh-jist) a scientist who learns about ancient times by studying things he or she digs up, such as old buildings, tools, and pottery

artifacts (ART-uh-*fakts*) objects of historical interest that were made by people

bacteria (bak-TEER-ee-uh) tiny living things; some bacteria are helpful, while others can cause disease

Book of the Dead (BUK UHV THUH DED) a collection of ancient Egyptian spells and prayers meant to guide the dead into the afterlife

burial chamber (BER-ee-uhl CHAYM-bur) a room where a dead body is placed

collectors (kuh-LEK-turz) people who gather and keep pieces of artwork or other interesting objects

curse (KURSS) something that brings or causes evil or misfortune

customs (KUSS-tuhmz) the usual ways of doing things

embalmers (em-BAHM-urz) people who work to preserve dead bodies

experts (EK-spurts) people who know a lot about a subject

fragile (FRAJ-il) easily broken or damaged

internal organs (in-TUR-nuhl OR-guhnz) body parts that do particular jobs and are found inside the body

molds (MOHLDZ) plant-like living things that grow in old food and on damp surfaces

mummy (MUH-mee) the preserved body of a dead person or animal

pharaoh (FAIR-oh) ruler of ancient Egypt

pyramids (PEER-uh-midz) stone buildings with a square base and triangular sides that meet at a point on top

sacred (SAY-krid) holy, religious

sarcophagus (sar-KOF-uh-guhss) a stone box made for holding a coffin

sealed (SEELD) closed up

supernatural (*soo*-pur-NACH-ur-uhl) having to do with something unusual that breaks the laws of nature

superstition (*soo*-pur-STI-shuhn) a belief based on the fear of the unknown

suspense (suh-SPENSS) a feeling of uncertainty while waiting for something to happen

tablet (TAB-lit) a flat object with writing carved on it

temples (TEM-puhlz) religious buildings where people come to pray

tomb (TOOM) a grave, room, or building in which a dead body is buried

toxins (TOKS-inz) poisons

vengeful (VENJ-fuhl) seeking punishment for something that has been unfairly done

Bibliography

Handwerk, Brian. "Egypt's 'King's Tut's Curse' Caused by Tomb Toxins?" *National Geographic News* (May 6, 2005).

Hawass, Zahi. *The Golden King: The World of Tutankhamun.* Washington, D.C.: National Geographic (2004).

Reeves, Nicholas. *The Complete Tutankhamun: The King, the Tomb, the Royal Treasure.* London: Thames and Hudson (1990).

Woods, Michael and Mary B. *The Tomb of King Tutankhamen.* Minneapolis, MN: Twenty-First Century Books (2008).

Read More

Briscoe, Diana. *King Tut: Tales from the Tomb.* Mankato, MN: Capstone (2003).

Hawass, Zahi. *Tutankhamun: The Mystery of the Boy King.* Washington, D.C.: National Geographic (2005).

Landau, Elaine. *The Curse of Tutankhamen.* Brookfield, CT: Millbrook (1996).

Reeves, Nicholas. *Into the Mummy's Tomb: The Real-Life Discovery of Tutankhamun's Treasures.* New York: Scholastic (1992).

Zoehfeld, Kathleen Weidner. *The Curse of King Tut's Mummy.* New York: Random House (2007).

Learn More Online

To learn more about King Tut and his tomb, visit
www.bearportpublishing.com/HorrorScapes

Index

About the Author

Natalie Lunis has written many nonfiction books for children. She recently encountered mummies in New York City—at the Metropolitan Museum of Art and the Brooklyn Museum.